Hikin... Foothills Trail

White blazes lead the way on the Foothills Trail.

Hiking South Carolina's
Foothills Trail

Scott Lynch

milestone press

almond, nc

Milestone Press, P.O. Box 158, Almond, NC 28702
www.milestonepress.com

Book design by Jim Parham

Cover photographs by Jim Parham, Thomas King, and the author.
Interior photographs by the author unless otherwise indicated.

Library of Congress Cataloging-in-Publication Data

Lynch, Scott, 1973–
 Hiking South Carolina's Foothills Trail / Scott Lynch.
    pages cm
 Summary: "A concise guide to South Carolina's Foothills
National Recreation Trail. Includes detailed trail maps, complete
driving and hiking directions, trailheads with GPS coordinates,
recommendations for thru-hiking, and suggestions for day and
overnight hikes"–Provided by publisher.
  ISBN 978-1-889596-30-3 (alk. paper)
  1. Hiking–South Carolina–Guidebooks. 2. Trails–South
Carolina–Guidebooks. 3. South Carolina–Guidebooks. I. Title.
  GV199.42.S58L965 2015
    796.5109757–dc23
                        2014048131

Printed in the United States on recycled paper

This book is dedicated to my father, Dr. Cletus E. Lynch, who introduced me to camping when I was a young boy. Thank you for taking me places, and always saying you're proud of me. I love you, POPS!

Table of Contents

West to East: Oconee to Table Rock

The Crown Jewel: Laurel Valley to Bad Creek

Top 10 Backpacking Overnights

Top 10 Day Hikes

You'll cross over and hike beside five different rivers along the Foothills Trail.

Introduction

The Foothills Trail is a 76.2-mile hiking path that begins and ends in South Carolina, crossing the North Carolina state line twice between its eastern terminus at Table Rock State Park and its western terminus at Oconee State Park. It passes through the South Carolina counties of Pickens and Oconee and the North Carolina counties of Transylvania and Jackson.

The trail can be hiked in either direction. It climbs over Sassafras Mountain, South Carolina's highest point, and passes through Laurel Valley Heritage Preserve; the Andrew Pickens Ranger District of Sumter National Forest; and Ellicott Rock Wilderness. It skirts beautiful Lake Jocassee and crosses the Toxaway, Horsepasture, Thompson, Whitewater and Chattooga rivers, passing Virginia Hawkins Falls, Laurel Fork Falls, Hilliard Falls, Whitewater Falls (highest waterfall east of the Mississippi), King Creek Falls, and Pigpen and Licklog Falls.

This National Recreation Trail, maintained by the Foothills Trail Conference, offers nearly endless options for a true backcountry experience. You can choose day hikes of varying difficulty, overnight backpacking trips starting and ending at different access points, or a thru-hike of the entire trail. Its "crown jewel" is a 3-day section between Laurel Valley and Bad Creek, considered one of the best long-weekend backpacking trips in the Southeast. Once you begin adventures on the Foothills Trail, you're likely to return again and again.

Planning Your Hike

What to Expect

The Foothills Trail offers a rugged backcountry experience where thru-hikers encounter strenuous hiking each day. Water sources are plentiful (but be prepared to filter and/or purify drinking water) and there are many established campsites, but no shelters on the trail—so pack a tent, hammock, tarp, or bivy. Weather can change frequently in any season, so always be prepared with season-specific clothing layers.

Using this Guide

This guide provides concise trail data for hiking from Table Rock to Oconee (east to west) and Oconee to Table Rock (west to east), including suggestions for where to camp when thru-hiking; the best overnight hikes; the best day hikes; and details on the 3-day "crown jewel" section from Laurel Valley to Bad Creek.

The mileage data in this guide has been verified against existing historical data, and with GPS tracking. The first page of every hiking section includes a rough elevation profile at the top.

Take this guide with you on your Foothills Trail adventures, and be sure to read ahead! Before setting out, learn the symbols and notations used throughout the book, and thoroughly familiarize yourself with your destination and with water sources, campsites, landmarks, and waypoints you'll encounter as you go.

Backcountry Camping Gear Checklist

To Carry

- Shelter: tent, tarp, hammock, or bivy; tent stakes
- Backpack with rain cover
- Sleeping bag, pad, and camp pillow
- Properly fitted hiking footwear
- Water filtration/purification system
- Clean water container (hydration bladder, bottle)
- Headlamp and extra batteries
- Trekking poles
- 3 ways to make fire and tinder
- Stove and fuel
- Cook pot, cup, and eating utensils
- Food and snacks for each day
- Bag for trash
- First aid kit
- Emergency whistle
- Personal hygiene items and medications
- Small roll of duct tape
- Toilet paper and trowel
- Hand sanitizer and biodegradable soap
- Sunscreen and lip balm
- Insect repellent (if season requires)
- Quick-dry towel
- Stuff sacks
- Resealable small plastic bags
- 550-style small tie cord
- Waterproof wristwatch
- Small pocket knife
- Compass (and know how to use it)
- Small thermal safety blanket
- Camera
- Reading material; writing pad and pen
- Identification
- Folding camp chair
- Car keys
- *Hiking South Carolina's Foothills Trail* Pocket Guide

Backcountry Camping Gear Checklist (continued)

To Wear
- ☐ Sun protection/warm hat
- ☐ Sunglasses with neck cord
- ☐ Bandanna
- ☐ Season-specific layering clothing
- ☐ Quick-dry clothing (no cotton)
- ☐ Rain shell
- ☐ Camp shoes
- ☐ Spare socks (woolen or synthetic)

Other
- ☐ Dry clothes and towel (to keep in car)
- ☐ Small bills for parking/entry fees
- ☐ Provide itinerary to family/friends

Outfitters Near the Foothills Trail

The following outdoor specialty outfitters can help you gear up for your Foothills Trail adventures. Always seek professional advice for your backcountry gear choices.

- Appalachian Outfitters, Greenville, SC 864-987-0618
- Grady's Great Outdoors, Anderson, SC 864-226-5283
- Half-Moon Outfitters, Greenville, SC 864-233-4001
- Outdoor Adventures, Clemson, SC 864-653-9007
- REI, Greenville, SC 864-297-0588
- Sunrift Adventures, Travelers Rest, SC 864-834-3019
- The Local Hiker, Spartanburg, SC 864-764-1651

Resources

Due to its remote location, there is typically no cell phone service on the Foothills Trail. However, sometimes on exposed ridges and at some of the trailheads, depending on weather, some cell phones may get a signal. Be sure to leave your itinerary (including copies of this guide) with family and friends. The following is a list of relevant contacts.

- SC Dept. of Natural Resources (DNR) 803-922-5431
- DNR Jocassee Field Office....................... 864-878-9071
- NC Wildlife Resource Commission 919-707-0010
- USDA Forest Service SC 864-638-9568
- USDA Forest Service NC 828-524-6441
- Oconee County, SC............................... 864-638-4111
- Pickens County, SC 864-898-5500
- Transylvania County, NC......................... 828-884-3168
- Jackson County, NC............................... 828-586-1911
- Oconee State Park................................. 864-638-5353
- Table Rock State Park 864-878-9813
- Gorges State Park 828-966-9099
- Foothills Trail Conference .... www.foothillstrail.org
- Duke Energy (Bad Creek Office)................ 864-944-2308

Getting to the Trailheads

Directions to the Major Trailheads

Eastern Terminus—Table Rock State Park
864-878-9813
GPS 35.031852, -82.700344

From Greenville, SC, drive north on SC 276, passing through the towns of Travelers Rest, Marietta, and Cleveland. At the intersection with SC 11, continue straight on SC 11 and drive 8.9 miles. At the sign for Table Rock State Park, turn right on West Gate Road and drive 0.5 miles to the Table Rock State

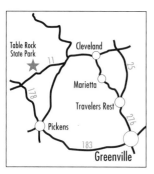

Park entrance and fee station. Continue 0.7 mile into the park to the large parking lot to the right. The Foothills Trail starts at the Interpretative Center across from the parking area (it shares the trailhead with Table Rock Trail).

Note: There is a fee to enter this state park.

Western Terminus—Oconee State Park
864-638-5353
GPS 34.86051, -83.097947

From Walhalla, SC, drive
north on SC 28 for 8.3 miles
and turn right (north) on SC
107. Drive approximately 2.3
miles to the Oconee State Park
entrance and fee station. Enter
and follow signs another mile
to Foothills Trail trailhead.

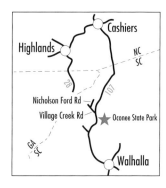

Note: There is a fee to enter
this state park.

Laurel Valley Access
864-878-9071 (DNR Jocassee Field Office)
GPS 35.048479, -82.814813

From Pickens, SC, drive north on SC 178 for approximately 9
miles to the 4-way stop at SC 11. Continue straight on SC 178
and drive 8 miles to the Rocky Bottom area, crossing over the
bridge. The Foothills Trail crosses here and follows gravel Horse-

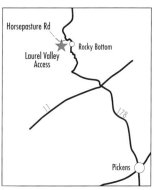

pasture Road uphill. Make a
left on Horsepasture Road,
continue for 0.3 mile, and park
at the large gravel parking
area with the sign for Laurel
Valley Access. Walk down the
road for 100 feet and Foothills
Trail re-enters the woods to the
right, ascending steep wooden
steps.

Bad Creek Access
864-944-4000
GPS 35.011846, -82.999767

From Salem, SC, drive north on SC130 for 1.3 miles to its intersection with SC 11. Continue straight on SC 130 (Whitewater Falls Road) for 10.8 miles and turn right at Duke Power's Bad Creek Hydroelectric Station on Bad Creek Road. This is a gated entrance open from 6 am to 6 pm (but you may exit at any time). Drive 2.1 miles and turn left on Bad Creek Road, following signs for Foothills Trail to a large parking area. The trailhead, marked by a sign, is on the far side of the parking lot.

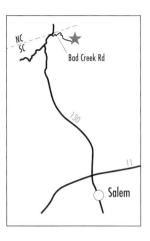

Burrell's Ford Access
864-638-9568 (Andrew Pickens Ranger Station, USFS)
GPS 34.971294, -83.114431

From Walhalla, SC, drive north on SC 28 for 8.3 miles and turn right (north) on SC 107. Drive approximately 10.1 miles. Turn left on gravel Burrell's Ford Road. Drive 2.3 miles to Burrell's Ford parking area on the left. The trailhead for Foothills Trail is on the left at the top of the parking area.

Directions to the Minor/Ancillary Trailheads

Sassafras Mountain Access
864-878-9071 (DNR Jocassee Field Office)
GPS 35.064575, -82.776146

From Pickens, SC, drive north on SC 178 for approximately 9 miles to the 4-way stop at SC 11. Continue straight on SC 178 for 7.2 miles and turn right on F. Van Clayton Memorial Highway. Drive 4.7 miles uphill to the Sassafras parking area. The Foothills Trail crosses the parking area.
Note: Sassafras Mountain is the highest point in South Carolina at 3,553 feet.

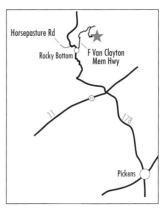

Sloan Bridge Access
864-638-9568 (Andrew Pickens Ranger Station, USFS)
GPS 34.971294, -83.114431

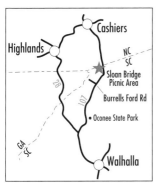

From Walhalla, SC, drive north on SC 28 for 8.3 miles and turn right (north) on SC 107. Drive approximately 14.2 miles and bear left into Sloan Bridge parking and picnic area. The Foothills Trail crosses over SC 107 here and continues on the far side of the picnic area.

Nicholson Ford Road Access
864-638-9568 (Andrew Pickens Ranger Station, USFS)
GPS 34.920836, -83.121357

From Walhalla, SC, drive north on SC 28 for 8.3 miles and turn right (north) on SC 107. Drive 3.1 miles, passing the entrance to Oconee State Park, and turn left on Village Creek Road. Drive

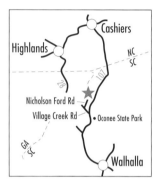

1.7 miles and turn right on Nicholson Ford Road. This road is gravel and fords a couple of trickling brooks; vehicles with low clearance could have difficulty crossing after heavy rains. Drive 2.2 miles on Nicholson Ford Road to the parking area, where Foothills Trail crosses.

Cheohee Road Access
864-638-9568 (Andrew Pickens Ranger Station, USFS)
GPS 34.914542, -83.110416

From Walhalla, SC, drive north on SC 28 for 8.3 miles and turn right (north) on SC 107. Continue 6.1 miles and turn right on gravel Cheohee Road (also called Winding Stairs Road). It is about 600 feet to the Cheohee Road access parking on the right.

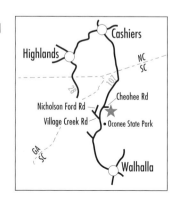

Gorges State Park–Canebrake Trail & Auger Trail Access
828-966-9099
GPS 35.108573, -82.883144

From Rosman, NC, drive north on NC 178 for 0.8 mile to the intersection with NC 64. Turn left on NC 64, continue 1.5 miles, and turn left on Frozen Creek Road. Drive 3.0 miles and turn right into the gravel parking area for Gorges State Park Canebrake and Auger trailheads. Canebrake Trail intersects with Foothills Trail at the top of Jocassee/Toxaway in approximately 5 miles.

Important: These directions are for *hiking* access from the Canebrake Trail in Gorges State Park, NC, not to be confused with the popular Canebrake boat access.

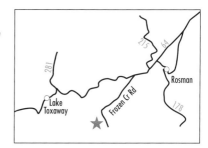

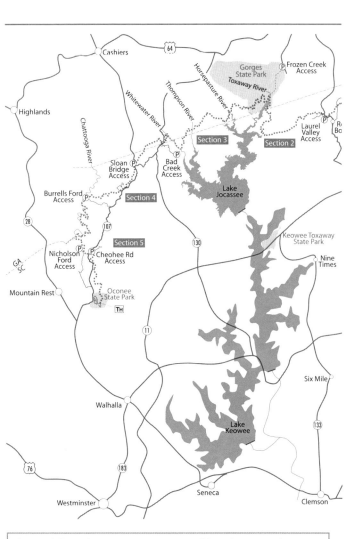

The Foothills Trail is easy to navigate. It is blazed WHITE. Blazes generally are spaced 30 seconds to a couple of minutes apart when hiking. A double blaze indicates the trail is making a nonintuitive turn. When you encounter a double blaze, stop, look around, and find the next blaze.

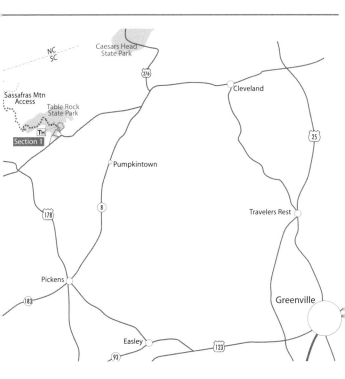

Legend

▪ ▪ ▪	....	Foothills Trail
- - -	....	other trail
▬	....	paved road
─	....	dirt road
△	....	summit
🌊	....	waterfall
◉	....	of interest
Δ	....	campsite
♦	....	water source
TH	....	trailhead
Ⓟ	....	parking area
⑪	....	state highway
🛈178	....	US highway

Note

In hiking directions, the distance from a water source to the next water source is given in parentheses, for example: Stream crossing, bridge (1.5 mi ♦).

A basic elevation profile for a trail section is at the very top of the first page for that section.

Table Rock Mountain looms high above its state park namesake.

East to West

Table Rock to Oconee

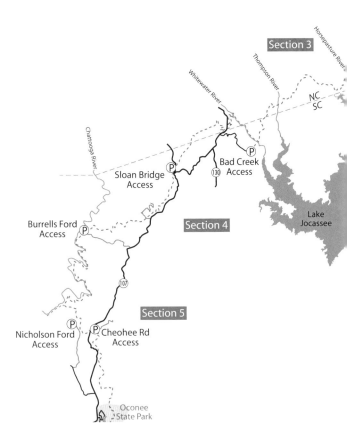

Thru-Hike Mileage and Camping Recommendations

5-Day Thru-Hike (average 15.3 miles per day)

Day 1* 8.6 miles: Table Rock State Park to
        John L. Cantrell homesite camping
Day 2   17.7 miles: John L. Cantrell homesite to Rock Creek
Day 3   15.5 miles: Rock Creek to Thompson River
Day 4   17.9 miles: Thompson River to Burrell's Ford
Day 5   16.5 miles: Burrell's Ford to Oconee State Park

6-Day Thru-Hike (average 12.7 miles per day)

Day 1*   8.6 miles: Table Rock State Park to
         John L. Cantrell homesite camping
Day 2   13.2 miles: John L. Cantrell homesite to
         Laurel Fork Falls
Day 3   11.8 miles: Laurel Fork Falls to Bear Creek
Day 4   16.2 miles: Bear Creek to Round Mountain
         spur trail camping
Day 5   12 miles: Round Mountain spur camping to
         Chattooga River valley
Day 6   14 miles: Chattooga River valley to
         Oconee State Park

7-Day Thru-Hike (average 10.8 miles per day)

Day 1*   8.6 miles: Table Rock State Park to
         John L. Cantrell homesite camping
Day 2   11 miles: John L. Cantrell homesite to
         Virginia Hawkins Falls area
Day 3   14 miles: Virginia Hawkins area to Bear Creek
Day 4   10.3 miles: Bear Creek to camping east of
         Bad Creek
Day 5   15.8 miles: East of Bad Creek to Burrell's Ford
Day 6   8.1 miles: Burrell's Ford to Pigpen Falls area
Day 7   8.4 miles: Pigpen Falls area to Oconee State Park

* Lower mileage for Day 1 allows time to shuttle vehicles.

Section 1
Table Rock State Park to Laurel Valley Access
Distance 14.5 miles

Section Miles	Directions	Cumulative Miles
0.0	Begin at Table Rock State Park Carrick Creek Interpretive Center. This is the Foothills Trail eastern terminus.	0.0
0.2	Trail is paved. Unlimited water sources in this general area. Cross 50-ft metal bridge over Carrick Creek. Junction with Table Rock Trail. Turn left (2.2 mi ♦).	0.2
0.9	Junction with Carrick Creek Trail; Foothills Trail bears left. You are officially on Pinnacle Mountain Trail (yellow blaze).	0.9
2.4	50-ft low-flow waterfall on right (0.9 mi ♦).	2.4
2.6	Junction with Mill Creek Falls spur. Trail turns hard right.	2.6

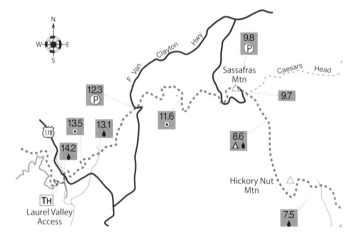

3.3	Cross Mill Creek (2.0 mi ♦). Trail turns right and begins ascending.	3.3
3.7	Large rock outcrop of Pinnacle Mountain (false summit) with expansive view of SC Upstate. Trail crosses top of rock, turns hard right, re-enters woods, and begins ascending. Watch for blazes.	3.7
4.1	Junction with Foothills Trail and first official marker, sign, and blazes. Turn left.	4.1

4.5	Boundary of Table Rock State Park. Trail descends. Downhill to the right is Drawbar Cliffs, a large rock outcrop with views to Lake Keowee. Small camping spot at top of rock close to trees.	4.5
5.0	"Lighthouse" cave. Small camping area.	5.0
5.3	Descend wooden steps. Cross small creek flowing over open rock (0.7 mi ♦).	5.3
5.9	Piney Mountain Gap and gravel Rockhouse Rd.	5.9
6.0	Stream crossing, bridge (1.5 mi ♦).	6.0
6.6	Emory Gap Toll Rd. Greenville Watershed boundary (red blaze). Observe "no trespassing" signs.	6.6
7.5	Stream crossing, bridge (1.1 mi ♦).	7.5
8.6	**End Day 1 of All Thru-Hikes** Chimney remains of John L. Cantrell homesite. Small camping area. Water source 200 ft beyond old chimney (4.5 mi ♦).	**8.6**
9.7	Spur trail to Caesars Head, behind red gate.	9.7
9.8	Summit of Sassafras Mountain (3,553 ft), highest point in SC.	9.8
11.6	Short side spur to Balancing Rock.	11.6
12.3	Chimney Top Gap, F. Van Clayton Hwy, large sign kiosk.	12.3
13.1	Stream crossing, bridge (1.1 mi ♦).	13.1
13.5	Big rock outcrop on right (north).	13.5
14.2	Cross SC 178, bridge. Water source below (2.0 mi ♦). Turn left and follow gravel road uphill.	14.2
14.5	Reach parking area with sign for Laurel Valley Access.	14.5

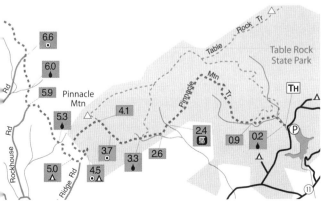

Section Miles	Directions	Cumulative Miles
0.0	From the Laurel Valley access parking area, walk down road 100 ft and trail re-enters woods to the right, ascending steep wooden steps. For next 0.5 mi, trail generally parallels road.	14.5
0.5	Trail steeply descends many wooden steps to Horsepasture Rd level, then ascends more wooden steps.	15.0
1.7	Cross 18-ft log bridge over small stream (0.9 mi ♦).	16.2
2.6	Large open camping area. Small stream nearby (1.2 mi ♦).	17.1
3.0	Cross gravel access road. Sign for Laurel Fork Heritage Preserve.	17.5
3.8	Enter Laurel Valley area by descending steeply, including steps. Over the next 3 miles, trail crosses Laurel Fork Creek many times, with abundant water sources and camping opportunities (0.7 mi ♦).	18.3

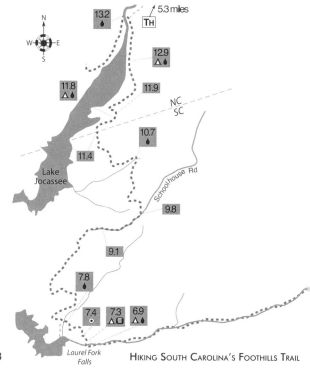

28   *Laurel Fork Falls*

4.5	**End Day 2 of 7-Day** Wooden bench. Trail descends steps to Virginia Hawkins Falls. Very small campsite. Be courteous when camping at this popular day-hiking destination (2.4 mi ♦).	**19.0**
6.9	Large camping area just before iron gate across dirt road. Trail turns left (0.4 mi ♦).	21.4
7.3	**End Day 2 of 6-Day** Short spur trail on left. Cross 75-ft suspension bridge to large Laurel Fork Creek/Falls camping area. Use extreme caution if exploring Laurel Fork Falls; people have fallen and died here (0.5 mi ♦).	**21.8**
7.4	Laurel Fork Falls overlook to the left.	21.9
7.8	Sign; 900-ft spur trail to left, descending to Lake Jocassee/ Laurel Fork boat access. Continue right. (2.9 mi ♦).	22.3
9.1	Iron gate, trail turns right. Trail stays close to, on, or above gravel Schoolhouse Rd for next 0.5 mi.	23.6
9.8	Iron gate, dirt road.	24.3
10.7	Stream crossing, bridge (1.1 mi ♦).	25.2
11.4	Sign for Gorges State Park. NC/SC state line.	25.9
11.8	**End Day 2 of 5-Day** Enter Rock Creek area. Cross 35-ft bridge over Rock Creek. Large camping spot (0.8 mi ♦).	**26.3**
11.9	Begin climbing "Heartbreak Ridge." For next 0.7 mi, ascend and descend hundreds of steps. This is widely considered the most difficult section of the entire Foothills Trail; hydrate and rest when needed.	26.4
12.9	Enter Toxaway/Jocassee area. Several excellent campsites over the next 0.3 mi. Unlimited water from lake.	27.4

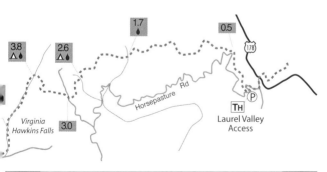

13.2	Intersection with 5-mi Canebrake Trail in Gorges State Park. Cross 225-ft suspension bridge over Toxaway River. Trail turns left, descends, and is at shore level for the next 0.3 mi.	27.7

Section 3
Jocassee/Toxaway to Bad Creek Access
Distance 16.8 miles

Section Miles	Directions	Cumulative Miles
0.0	Intersection with 5-mi Canebrake Trail in Gorges State Park. Cross 225-ft suspension bridge over Toxaway River. Trail turns left, descends, and stays at shore level for next 0.3 mi (0.4 mi ◆).	27.7
0.4	Canebrake boat access. Trail soon turns right, up and away from lake. For nearly the next mile, trail ascends steeply (1.3 mi ◆).	28.1
1.7	Stream crossing on two timbers (1.9 mi ◆).	29.4
3.6	Cross Cobb Creek; rock overhang, lush thicket (2.3 mi ◆).	31.3
4.9	Powerlines. Route intersects Auger Hole Trail; exit Gorges State Park.	32.6
5.9	**End Day 3 of 6-Day & 7-Day** Cross Bear Creek on 35-ft bridge. Large camping area on left (2.4 mi ◆).	**33.6**
7.2	Cross 50-ft suspension bridge over dry ravine. NO WATER.	34.9

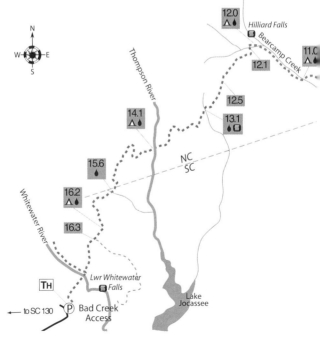

HIKING SOUTH CAROLINA'S FOOTHILLS TRAIL

8.3	Descend stairs, cross 115-ft bridge over Horsepasture River. When thru-hiking, this is widely considered the halfway point of Foothills Trail. For next 2.5 mi, trail follows old logging road (2.7 mi ◑).	36.0
11.0	Enter Bearcamp Creek area. Trail turns hard left. Walk through campsite, cross bridge. For next 1.1 mi, walk along Bearcamp Creek, with unlimited water sources and several camping areas.	38.7
12.0	Large camping area to the left. To right is 0.2-mi spur trail to Hilliard Falls. More camping near waterfall.	39.7
12.1	Cross Bearcamp Creek on steep 35-ft bridge (1.0 mi ◑).	39.8
12.5	Iron gate, cross gravel road. Ascend steps.	40.2

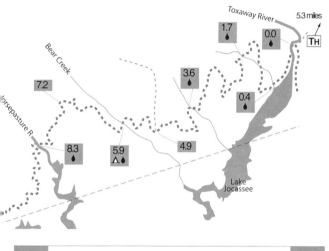

13.1	Stream crossing, small waterfall (1.0 mi ◑).	40.8
14.1	**End Day 3 of 5-Day** Cross Thompson River on 75-ft wooden bridge. Several camping spots on east side of bridge (1.5 mi ◑).	**41.8**
15.6	Stream crossing, bridge (0.6 mi ◑).	43.3
16.2	**End Day 4 of 7-Day** Follow sign to large campsite downhill to left. Campsite sign. Water source (0.6 mi ◑).	**43.9**
16.3	Trail comes to old logging road. Turn hard right, go 75 ft, turn hard left. (A left on this old logging road goes to Lower Whitewater Falls overlook, a 2-mi round trip.)	44.0
16.8	Trail junction with sign. **Foothills Trail continues right.** (Continue straight 0.7 mi to Duke Energy's Bad Creek access, parking, and portable toilets.)	44.5

Section Miles	Directions	Cumulative Miles
0.0	Trail junction with sign. **Foothills Trail continues right.** (Continue straight 0.7 mi to Duke Energy's Bad Creek access and parking with portable toilets.) For next 1.7 mi, walk along Whitewater River. Unlimited water sources. **No camping** is allowed on this section of trail.	44.5
1.7	Cross Whitewater River on 60-ft steel bridge; boulder field (2.1 mi ◆).	46.2
2.3	Spur trail to Upper Whitewater Falls overlook.	46.8
2.8	Spur trail to Whitewater Falls parking area and restroom.	47.3
3.1	Trail crosses NC 281, small parking area.	47.6
3.8	Stream crossing (1.5 mi ◆).	48.3
4.8	Benches, views of Lake Jocassee.	49.3

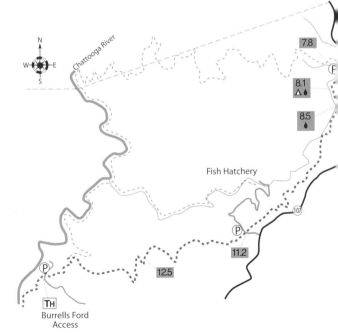

5.3	**End Day 4 of 6-Day** Quarter-mile spur trail with camping, which continues 1.4 mi to NC 281. Several water sources along spur (0.9 mi ◆).	**49.8**
6.2	Stream crossing (1.6 mi ◆).	50.7
6.4	NC/SC state line and sign.	50.9

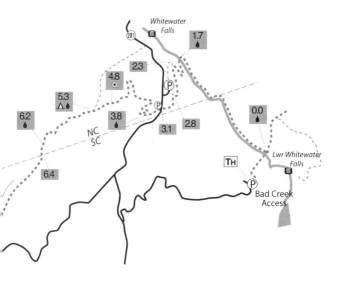

7.8	Trail crossing SC 107, Sloan Bridge Picnic Area, pit toilet, parking (0.3 mi ◆).	52.3
8.1	Campsite off-trail and downhill (0.4 mi ◆).	52.6
8.5	Cross 18-ft bridge; 50-ft sluice waterfall and steps (6.7 mi ◆).	53.0
11.2	Trail crosses Fish Hatchery Rd.	55.7
12.5	Begin descending into Chattooga River Gorge via switchbacks, which continue for 0.75 mi.	57.0
15.2	**End Day 4 of 5-Day & Day 5 of 7-Day** Cross gravel road to Burrell's Ford parking lot; pit toilet in parking lot. Follow sign to Burrell's Ford Campground nearby. At top left of parking lot, trail re-enters the woods (0.5 mi ◆).	**59.7**

Section 5
Burrell's Ford to Oconee State Park
Distance 16.5 miles

Section Miles	Directions	Cumulative Miles
0.0	**End Day 4 of 5-Day & Day 5 of 7-Day** Burrell's Ford access. Pit toilet in parking lot. Burrell's Ford Campground nearby. Trail re-enters woods at top left of parking lot (0.5 mi ◐).	**59.7**
0.5	Spur trail to King Creek Falls. Turn hard right to continue on Foothills Trail (0.5 mi ◐).	60.2
1.0	**End Day 5 of 6-Day** Leaving Burrell's Ford area. Pass spur trail leading back to Burrell's Ford Campground, right 0.25 mi. Trail joins the Chattooga River; for next 4.9 mi the trail stays close to the river. Numerous water sources and camping opportunities; best campsites are in miles 62-63, along river.	**60.7**
5.9	Trail moves away from Chattooga River and stays away or above it for next 1.5 mi (blue blaze) (2.0 mi ◐).	65.6
7.4	Outer boundary of Chattooga Wild and Scenic River area.	67.1
8.1	**End Day 6 of 7-Day** Signs. Trail curves to left and continues straight. Pigpen Falls area; plenty of water and camping here (0.2m ◐). Pigpen Falls is below and to your right.	**67.8**
8.3	Cross Licklog Creek on long telephone pole bridge; abundance of water/camping in this area (0.9 mi ◐).	68.0
8.9	Cross through gravel Nicholson Ford Rd parking area. Trail re-enters woods at end of parking area to the left.	68.6
9.2	Three small bridge/stream crossings within 0.3 mi (3.3 mi ◐).	68.9
10.4	Cross SC 107 at Cheohee Rd (also called Winding Stairs Rd). Designated parking area 600 ft down the road.	70.1
11.9	Arrive at SC 107 at Jumping Brand Trailhead. Do not cross highway; trail re-enters woods straight ahead and to left. Very small parking area.	71.6
12.8	Cross stream on bridge with handrails (0.5 mi ◐).	72.5
13.3	Cross stream on bridge with handrails (3.2 mi ◐).	73.0
16.1	Cross gravel Station Mountain Rd. Trail to Tamassee Knob.	75.8
16.5	End at Oconee State Park, western terminus of Foothills Trail.	76.2

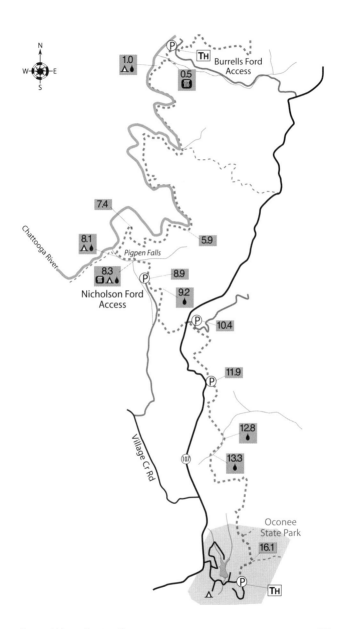

Steps like these are a common sight along the Foothills Trail.

West to East

Oconee to Table Rock

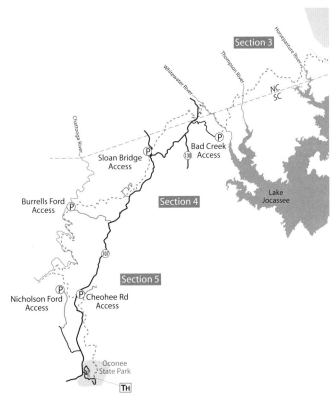

Thru-Hike Mileage and Camping Recommendations

5-Day Thru-Hike (average 15.3 miles per day)

Day 1* 12 miles: Oconee State Park to
        Chattooga River valley
Day 2   14 miles: Chattooga River valley to
        Round Mountain spur camping
Day 3   16.2 miles: Round Mountain spur camping to
        Bear Creek
Day 4   16.5 miles: Bear Creek to beyond
        Laurel Valley camping
Day 5   17.1 miles: beyond Laurel Valley to
        Table Rock State Park

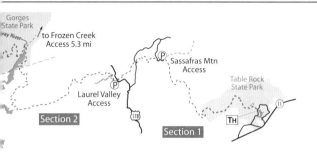

6-Day Thru-Hike (average 12.7 miles per day)

Day 1*	8.4 miles: Oconee State Park to Pigpen Falls area
Day 2	15.2 miles: Pigpen Falls area to just before Sloan Bridge camping
Day 3	12.8 miles: Sloan Bridge to Bearcamp Creek
Day 4	12.1 miles: Bearcamp Creek to head of Jocassee/Toxaway
Day 5	10.6 miles: head of Jocassee/Toxaway to beyond Laurel Valley camping
Day 6	17.1 miles: beyond Laurel Valley to Table Rock State Park

7-Day Thru-Hike (average 10.8 miles per day)

Day 1*	8.4 miles: Oconee State Park to Pigpen Falls area
Day 2	8.1 miles: Pigpen Falls area to Burrell's Ford
Day 3	15.8 miles: Burrell's Ford to camping beyond Bad Creek
Day 4	10.3 miles: beyond Bad Creek to Bear Creek
Day 5	11.8 miles: Bear Creek to Laurel Fork Falls
Day 6	13.6 miles: Laurel Fork Falls to John L. Cantrell homesite camping
Day 7	8.6 miles: John L. Cantrell homesite to Table Rock State Park

* Lower mileage for Day 1 allows time to shuttle vehicles.

Section 5
Oconee State Park to Burrell's Ford
Distance 16.5 miles

Section Miles	Directions	Cumulative Miles
0.0	Oconee State Park, western terminus of Foothills Trail (3.2 mi ◐).	0.0
0.4	Cross gravel Station Mountain Rd. Trail to Tamassee Knob.	0.4
3.2	Cross stream on bridge with handrails (0.5 mi ◐).	3.2
3.7	Cross stream on bridge with handrails (3.3 mi ◐).	3.7
4.6	Arrive at SC 107 at Jumping Brand Trailhead. Do not cross highway; trail re-enters woods straight ahead to the right. Very small parking area.	4.6
6.1	Cross SC 107 at Cheohee Road (also called Winding Stairs Rd). Designated parking area 600 ft back down Cheohee Road.	6.1
7.0	Three small bridge/stream crossings within 0.3 mi (1.2 mi ◐).	7.0
7.6	Cross through gravel Nicholson Ford Rd parking area.	7.6
8.2	Cross Licklog Creek over long telephone pole bridge; abundance of water and camping here (0.2 mi ◐).	8.2
8.4	**End Day 1 of 6-Day & 7-Day** Pigpen Falls area; abundance of water and camping here (2.0 mi ◐). Pigpen Falls is below and to your left; continue straight. Signs. After descending into valley, trail curves to right and moves away from Chattooga River (on your left, below).	**8.4**
9.1	Boundary of Chattooga Wild and Scenic River area (blue blaze). Trail continues away from Chattooga River.	9.1
10.6	**End Day 1 of 5-Day** Trail joins the Chattooga River. For next 4.9 mi, you are never more than a few minutes away from the river, with numerous water sources and camping opportunities. (Best campsites are in miles 12-14, along river.)	**10.6**
15.5	Enter Burrell's Ford area. Pass spur trail leading to Burrell's Ford Campground, 0.25 mi on left.	15.5
16.0	Spur trail to King Creek Falls. Turn hard left across bridge to continue on Foothills Trail (0.5 mi ◐).	16.0
16.5	**End Day 2 of 7-Day** Burrell's Ford access. Pit toilet in parking lot; Burrell's Ford Campground nearby. Trail continues across road and re-enters woods.	**16.5**

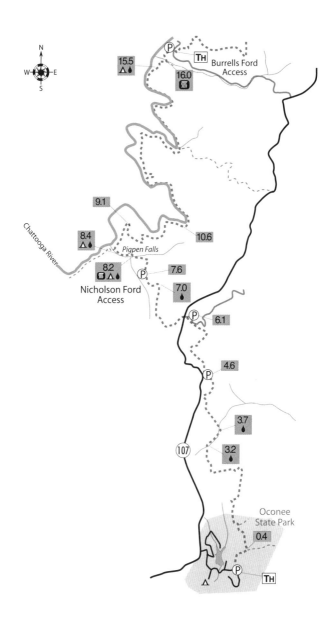

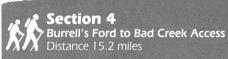

Section 4
Burrell's Ford to Bad Creek Access
Distance 15.2 miles

Section Miles	Directions	Cumulative Miles
0.0	**End Day 2 of 7-Day** Burrell's Ford access/gravel parking lot. Pit toilet in parking lot. For camping, follow signs to Burrell's Ford Campground nearby. Trail continues across road and re-enters woods.	**16.5**
2.0	Switchbacks out of Chattooga River Gorge; switchbacks continue for 0.75 mi.	18.5
4.0	Trail crosses Fish Hatchery Rd.	20.5
6.7	Cross 18-ft bridge; 50-ft sluice waterfall, steps (0.4 mi ♦).	23.2
7.1	**End Day 2 of 6-Day** Campsite off trail, downhill (0.3 mi ♦).	**23.6**
7.4	SC 107, Sloan Bridge Picnic Area, pit toilet, parking (1.6 mi ♦).	23.9
8.8	NC/SC state line and sign.	25.3

9.0	Stream crossing (0.9 mi ♦).	25.5
9.9	**End Day 2 of 5-Day** Quarter-mile spur trail continues 1.4 mi to NC 281; several water sources and camping along spur (1.5 mi ♦).	**26.4**
10.4	Benches, views of Lake Jocassee.	26.9
11.4	Stream crossing (2.1 mi ♦).	27.9

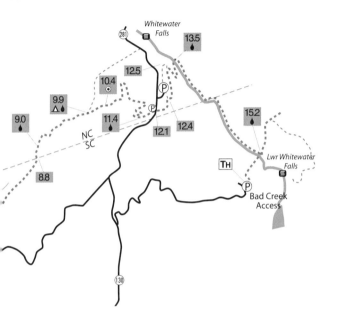

12.1	Trail crossing NC 281, small parking area.	28.6
12.4	Spur trail to Whitewater Falls parking and restroom.	28.9
12.5	Spur trail to Upper Whitewater Falls overlook.	29.0
13.5	Boulder field; cross Whitewater River on 60-ft steel bridge. For next 1.7 mi, walk along Whitewater River. Unlimited water sources. **No camping** is allowed on this section of trail.	30.0
15.2	T-junction with sign. **Foothills Trail continues left** (0.6 mi ♦). Right turn takes you 0.7 mi to Duke Energy's Bad Creek access/ parking with portable toilets.	31.7

Section 3
Bad Creek Access to Jocassee/Toxaway
Distance 16.8 miles

Section Miles	Directions	Cumulative Miles
0.0	Duke Energy's Bad Creek access/parking has portable toilets. Follow the access trail 0.7 mi to continue east on Foothills Trail (0.6 mi ♦).	31.7
0.5	Reach old logging road. Turn hard right, go 75 ft, turn hard left. (Continuing straight leads to Lower Whitewater Falls overlook.)	32.2
0.6	**End Day 3 of 7-Day** Follow sign to large campsite downhill to right. Water source (0.6 mi ♦).	**32.3**
1.2	Stream crossing, bridge (1.5 mi ♦).	32.9
2.7	Cross Thompson River on 75-ft wooden bridge. Several camping spots on east side of bridge (1.0 mi ♦).	34.4
3.7	Stream crossing, small waterfall (1.0 mi ♦).	35.4
4.3	Descend steps, cross gravel road, iron gate.	36.0
4.7	**End Day 3 of 6-Day** Cross Bearcamp Creek on 35-ft bridge. Large camping area past bridge to right. For next 1.1 mi, walk along Bearcamp Creek. Unlimited water, several camping spots.	**36.4**

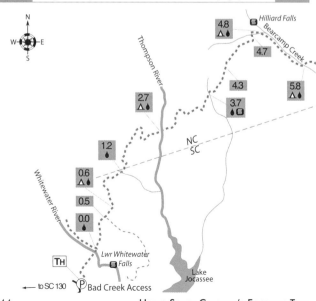

HIKING SOUTH CAROLINA'S FOOTHILLS TRAIL

4.8	To left is 0.2-mi spur trail to Hilliard Falls. More camping near waterfall.	36.5
5.8	After crossing third bridge and passing through campsite, trail turns hard right. For next 2.5 mi, trail follows old logging road (2.7 mi ♦).	37.5
8.5	Descend steps, cross 115-ft bridge over Horsepasture River. When thru-hiking, this river crossing is widely considered the halfway point of Foothills Trail (2.4 mi ♦).	40.2
9.6	Cross 50-ft suspension bridge over dry ravine. NO WATER.	41.3
10.9	**End Day 3 of 5-Day & Day 4 of 7-Day** Enter Bear Creek. Large camping spot to right. Cross Bear Creek on 35-ft bridge (2.3 mi ♦).	**42.6**
11.9	Powerlines; route intersects Auger Hole Trail in Gorges State Park.	43.6

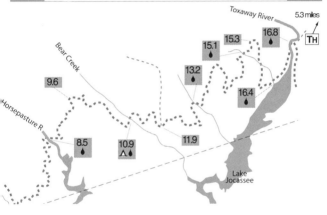

13.2	Cross Cobb Creek; rock overhang, lush thicket (1.9 mi ♦).	44.9
15.1	Stream crossing on two timbers (1.3 mi ♦).	46.8
15.3	For nearly the next mile, descend steeply into Lake Jocassee area.	47.0
16.4	Arrive at Lake Jocassee: trail nearly shore level with lake. Turn left; Canebrake boat access in approximately 0.1 mi. Unlimited water for the next mile as you traverse the head of Jocassee/Toxaway.	48.1
16.8	**End Day 4 of 6-Day** Cross 225-ft suspension bridge over Toxaway River; junction with 5-mi Canebrake Trail in Gorges State Park. Several excellent campsites in the 0.3 mi beyond bridge (0.8 mi ♦).	**48.5**

Section 2
Jocassee/Toxaway to Laurel Valley Access
Distance 13.2 miles

Section Miles	Directions	Cumulative Miles
0.0	**End Day 4 of 6-Day** Junction with 5-mi Canebrake Trail. Six large campsites over next 0.3 mi (0.8 mi ⬥).	**48.5**
0.6	Begin climbing "Heartbreak Ridge." For next 0.7 mi, ascend and descend hundreds of steps. This is widely considered the most difficult section of the entire Foothills Trail; hydrate and rest when needed.	49.1
1.8	Enter Rock Creek area; large camping spot. Cross Rock Creek on 35-ft. bridge (1.2 mi ⬥).	50.3
2.5	Sign for Gorges State Park. NC/SC state line.	51.0
3.4	Stream crossing, bridge (2.9 mi ⬥).	51.9
3.6	Iron gate. Trail stays close to, on, or above gravel Schoolhouse Rd for next 0.5 mi.	52.1

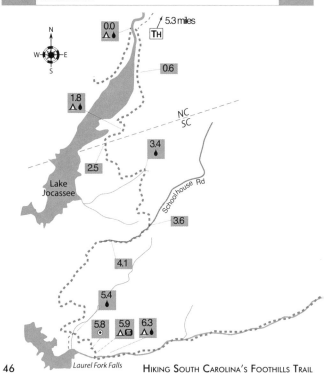

HIKING SOUTH CAROLINA'S FOOTHILLS TRAIL

4.1	Trail turns left; iron gate.	52.6
5.4	Continue straight/left. Sign; 900-ft spur trail to the right descends to Lake Jocassee/Laurel Fork boat access (0.7 mi ◆).	53.9
5.8	Laurel Fork Falls overlook to the right.	54.3
5.9	**End Day 5 of 7-Day** Short spur trail on right. Cross 75-ft suspension bridge to Laurel Fork Creek/Falls and large camping area. Use extreme caution if exploring Laurel Fork Falls; people have fallen and died here (0.4 mi ◆).	**54.4**
6.3	Iron gate, gravel road. Trail turns right. Large camping area to the right. For the next 3 miles, the trail crosses Laurel Fork Creek many times over bridges, timbers, and rocks. Unlimited water sources and many camping opportunities.	54.8
8.7	Virginia Hawkins Falls and very small campsite. Be courteous if camping at this popular day-hiking destination. Ascend steps.	57.2
9.4	Leave Laurel Fork Creek by ascending steps and continuing steep climb out of the valley (1.2 mi ◆).	57.9
10.2	Sign for Laurel Fork Heritage Preserve. Cross gravel access road.	58.7
10.6	**End Day 4 of 5-Day & Day 5 of 6-Day** Large, flat, open area with designated camping; small stream nearby (0.9 mi ◆).	**59.1**
11.5	Cross 18-ft log bridge over small stream (2.0 mi ◆).	60.0
12.7	Trail steeply descends many wooden steps to Horsepasture Rd level, then ascends wooden steps. For next 0.5 mi, trail generally parallels road.	61.2
13.2	Reach large gravel parking area with signs for Laurel Valley Access.	61.7

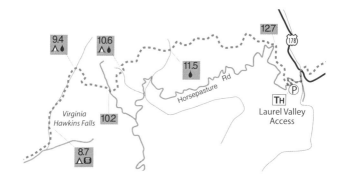

Section Miles	Directions	Cumulative Miles
0.0	Laurel Valley Access. From parking area, turn right (downhill), following gravel road.	61.7
0.3	Cross SC 178, bridge. Water source below (1.1 mi ◆).	62.0
1.0	Big rock outcrop on left (north).	62.7
1.4	Stream crossing, bridge (4.5 mi ◆).	63.1
2.2	Chimney Top Gap, F. Van Clayton Hwy; large sign kiosk.	63.9
2.9	Short side spur to Balancing Rock.	64.6
4.7	Summit of Sassafras Mountain (3,553-ft), highest point in SC.	66.4
4.8	Spur trail to Caesars Head, behind red gate.	66.5

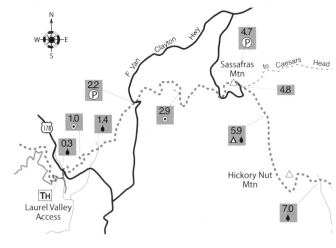

5.9	**End Day 6 of 7-Day** Chimney remains at John L. Cantrell homesite. Small camping spot. Water source 200 ft down beyond chimney (1.1 mi ◆).	**67.6**
7.0	Stream crossing, bridge (1.5 mi ◆).	68.7
7.9	Greenville Watershed boundary (red blaze); observe "no trespassing" signs. Emory Gap Toll Rd.	69.6

8.5	Stream crossing, bridge (0.7 mi 💧).	70.2
8.6	Piney Mountain Gap and gravel Rockhouse Rd.	70.3
9.2	Cross small creek flowing over open rock, ascend steps (2.0 mi 💧).	70.9
9.5	"Lighthouse" cave. Campsites.	71.2
10.0	To left is Drawbar Cliffs, a large rock outcrop with views to Lake Keowee. Small camping spot at top of rock close to trees. Trail climbs. Boundary of Table Rock State Park.	71.7
10.4	Junction with Pinnacle Trail (yellow blaze). End of the white blazes of Foothills Trail. Turn right, begin descending.	72.1
10.8	Open to large rock outcrop of Pinnacle Mountain (false summit) with expansive view of SC Upstate. Turn left; trail crosses top of rock, then descends into vegetation. Watch for blazes.	72.5
11.2	Cross Mill Creek (0.9 mi 💧).	72.9
11.9	Junction with Mill Creek Falls spur. Trail turns hard left.	73.6
12.1	50-ft low-flow waterfall on left (2.2 mi 💧).	73.8
13.6	Junction with Carrick Creek Trail; bear right.	75.3
14.3	Junction with Table Rock Trail; turn right. Cross 50-ft metal bridge over Carrick Creek. Trail is paved.	76.0
14.5	End at Table Rock State Park Carrick Creek Interpretive Center, eastern terminus of Foothills Trail.	76.2

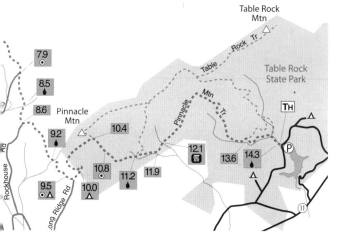

Laurel Fork Falls drops right into Lake Jocassee.

The "Crown Jewel"

Laurel Valley to Bad Creek

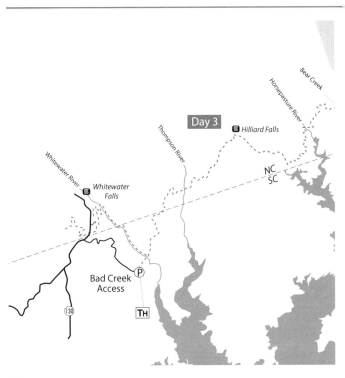

The "crown jewel" of the Foothills Trail is its 31-mile middle section from Laurel Valley to Bad Creek. This stretch may well be the best long weekend backpacking trip in the Carolinas. It can be hiked in either direction, but is most often hiked from east to west, beginning at Laurel Valley. *Directions here are for hiking east to west.*

Three-Day Mileage and Camping Recommendations

This 3-day, 2-night adventure offers the most remote hiking experience of the trail and should not be taken lightly. Plan for three hard days of backpacking at minimum. The recommended mileage breakdown by day is:

Day 1—7.3 miles with camping at Laurel Fork Falls
Day 2—11.8 miles with camping at Bear Creek
Day 3—11.6 miles

Lower mileage for Day 1 allows time to arrange shuttle vehicles.

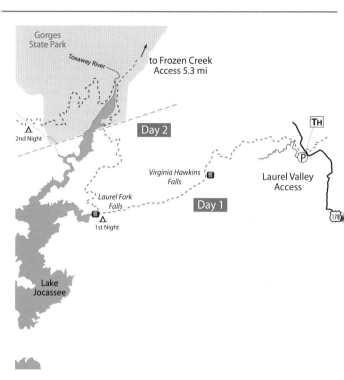

Foothills Trail is easy to navigate. Its white blazes generally are spaced 30 seconds to a few minutes apart when hiking. A double blaze indicates the trail is making a non-intuitive turn. When you encounter a double blaze, stop, look around, and find the next blaze.

Getting to the Trailheads
Laurel Valley Trailhead is off SC 178 at Rocky Bottom. Foothills Trail crosses the bridge and follows a gravel road uphill. Begin hiking at the large gravel parking area with signs for Laurel Valley Access.

Laurel Valley Trailhead
GPS 35.048479, -82.814813

Bad Creek Trailhead
GPS 35.011846, -82.999767

Day 1—Crown Jewel
Laurel Valley Access to Laurel Fork Falls
Distance 7.3 miles

Daily Miles	Directions	Cumulative Miles
0.0	Begin at large gravel parking area with sign for Laurel Valley Access. Walk down Horsepasture Rd for 100 ft; trail re-enters woods to the right, ascending steep wooden steps. For next 0.5 mi, trail generally parallels road.	0.0
0.5	Trail steeply descends many wooden steps to Horsepasture Rd level, then ascends more steeply wooden steps.	0.5
1.7	Cross 18-ft log bridge over small stream (0.9 mi ◖).	1.7
2.6	Large open area with designated camping, small stream nearby (1.2 mi ◖).	2.6
3.0	Cross gravel Canebrake Rd. Sign for Laurel Fork Heritage Preserve on right.	3.0
3.8	Descend steeply into Laurel Valley/Laurel Fork Creek area and reach valley floor. Over the next 3 mi, trail crosses Laurel Fork Creek many times on bridges, timbers, and rocks. Unlimited water and many camping opportunities here.	3.8
4.5	Wooden bench. Trail descends steps to Virginia Hawkins Falls and very small campsite.	4.5

7.3 △ ▨   6.9 △ ◖

Laurel Fork Falls

6.9	Large campsite, iron gate, dirt road. Trail turns left (0.4 mi ◐).	
		6.9
7.3	**End Day 1** Short spur trail on left. Cross 75-ft suspension bridge to Laurel Fork Creek/Falls camping area. Use caution if exploring Laurel Fork Falls; people have fallen and died here (0.5 mi ◐).	**7.3**

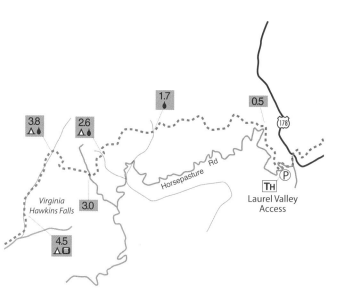

Day 2—Crown Jewel
Laurel Fork Falls to Bear Creek
Distance 11.8 miles

Daily Miles	Directions	Cumulative Miles
0.0	Cross 75-ft suspension bridge to leave camping area. Turn left. Use extreme caution if exploring near/top of Laurel Fork Falls; people have fallen and died here (0.5 mi ♦).	7.3
0.1	Laurel Fork Falls overlook to the left.	7.4
0.5	Sign and 900-ft spur trail to left, descending to Lake Jocassee/ Laurel Fork boat access. Continue right. (2.9 mi ♦).	7.8
1.8	Iron gate; trail turns right and stays close to gravel Schoolhouse Rd for next 0.5 mi.	9.1
2.5	Iron gate, dirt road.	9.8
3.4	Stream crossing, bridge (1.1 mi ♦).	10.7
4.1	Sign for Gorges State Park. NC/SC state line.	11.4
4.5	Enter Rock Creek area. Cross Rock Creek on 35-ft bridge; large camping area. (0.8 mi ♦).	11.8
4.6	Begin climbing "Heartbreak Ridge." For next 0.7 mi, ascend and descend hundreds of steps. Extremely strenuous; widely considered the most difficult section of entire Foothills Trail. Take caution, hydrate, and rest when needed.	11.9
5.6	Enter Toxaway/Jocassee area. Several excellent campsites over next 0.3 mi. Unlimited water for the next mile as you traverse the head of Jocassee/Toxaway.	12.9
5.9	Intersection with 5-mi Canebrake Trail in Gorges State Park. After crossing 225-ft suspension bridge over Toxaway River, trail turns left, descends, and is at shore level for next 0.3 mi.	13.2
6.3	Canebrake boat access. Soon the trail turns right, ascending steeply up and away from Lake Jocassee for nearly the next mile (1.3 mi ♦).	13.6
7.6	Stream crossing on two timbers (1.9 mi ♦).	14.9

9.5	Cross Cobb Creek; rock overhang, lush thicket (2.3 mi ◆).	16.8
10.8	Powerlines. Foothills Trail intersects Auger Hole Trail; Gorges State Park.	18.1
11.8	**End Day 2** Cross 35-ft bridge over Bear Creek. Large camping area to left (2.4 mi ◆).	**19.1**

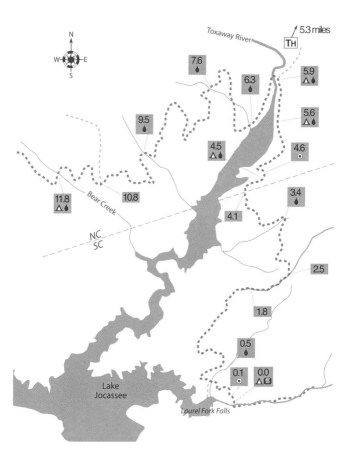

Day 3—Crown Jewel
Bear Creek to Bad Creek Access
Distance 11.6 miles

Daily Miles	Directions	Cumulative Miles
0.0	Leave Bear Creek campsite (2.4 mi ⬧).	19.1
1.3	Cross 50-ft suspension bridge over dry ravine. NO WATER.	20.4
2.4	Descend steps, cross 115-ft bridge over Horsepasture River. This is considered the halfway point of a Foothills Trail thru-hike. For the next 2.5 mi, trail follows old logging road (2.7 mi ⬧).	21.5
5.1	Enter Bearcamp Creek area; trail turns hard left. Walk through campsite, cross bridge. For next 1.1 mi, route follows Bearcamp Creek. Unlimited water sources and several campsites.	24.2

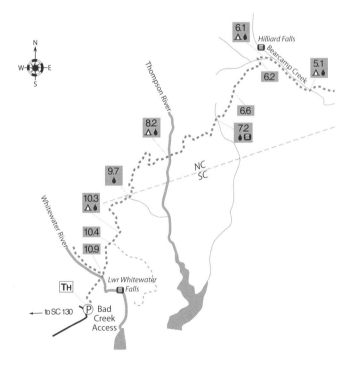

6.1	Large camping area to the left. On right is 0.2-mi spur trail to Hilliard Falls; more camping near waterfall.	25.2
6.2	Cross Bearcamp Creek on inclined 35-ft bridge (1.0 mi ◆).	25.3
6.6	Iron gate. Cross gravel road and ascend steps.	25.7
7.2	Stream crossing, small waterfall (1.0 mi ◆).	26.3
8.2	Cross 75-ft wooden bridge over Thompson River. Several camping spots on east side of bridge (1.5 mi ◆).	27.3

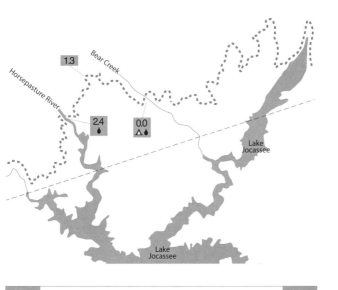

9.7	Stream crossing, bridge (0.6 mi ◆).	28.8
10.3	Large campsite and sign downhill to left. Water source (0.6 mi ◆).	29.4
10.4	Trail comes to old logging road; turn hard right, go 75-ft, turn hard left. (A left on this old logging road goes to Lower Whitewater Falls overlook.)	29.5
10.9	Trail junction with sign. Foothills Trail continues right. Follow signs toward Bad Creek Access. **Continue straight**, crossing two metal bridges over Whitewater River. After second bridge, turn left and follow trail through forest (blue blaze).	30.0
11.6	**End Day 3** Reach Duke Energy's Bad Creek Access parking area. Portable toilets here.	**30.7**

You can camp right next to the Chattooga River.

HIKING SOUTH CAROLINA'S FOOTHILLS TRAIL

Top 10 Backpacking Overnights

Easy

1. *Nicholson Ford Road Access to Pigpen Falls Area*
   Approximately1.5 miles each day, depending on campsite. Great for families with children or a quick overnighter. Offers the most camping space on the Foothills Trail. Also nearby: Licklog Falls and the Chattooga River.

2. *Burrell's Ford Area Camping*
   Up to 1 mile each day; for ease, the next best thing to car camping. Great for families with children or a quick overnighter. On holidays and warmer weather days, this camping area can be quite crowded. Arrive early!

Moderate

3. *Nicholson Ford Road Access to Chattooga River Valley*
   Between 3 and 6 miles each day, depending on campsite. You'll see many great campsites and waterfalls along the sometimes calm, sometimes turbulent Chattooga River.

4. *Burrell's Ford to Chattooga River*
   Between1.5 and 6 miles each day and easy-to-moderate depending on campsite selection; many great campsites. Within minutes you'll escape often crowded Burrell's Ford and experience some of the Chattooga's best scenery.

5. *Burrell's Ford to Pigpen Falls*
   8 miles each day. This is a great trip featuring the entire section of the Foothills Trail that follows the Chattooga River. Pigpen Falls' general area offers the most space of any camping on the Foothills Trail and suitable for large groups.

6. *Laurel Valley Access to Laurel Fork Falls*
   7.5 miles each day. Walk the entire length of Laurel Valley and see both Laurel Fork Falls and Virginia Hawkins Falls.

7. *Laurel Valley Access to Laurel Valley*
   4 to 6 miles each day, depending on campsite selection. Ascend through a dry hardwood forest, then head down into Laurel Valley's temperate rainforest. See Virginia Hawkins Falls and choose from abundant campsites.

Strenuous

8. *Bad Creek Access to Hilliard Falls/Bearcamp Creek Area*
   5.7 miles each day. Tough steep ascents and descents, including the beautiful Thompson River and lush Bearcamp Creek. Opportunities to camp right at Hilliard Falls, and practically unlimited camping along Bearcamp Creek.

9. *Bad Creek Access to Bear Creek*
   11.6 miles each day. Extremely strenuous; recommended for only the strongest backpackers. Cross over the steep ascents and descents of Thompson and Horsepasture Rivers, with hundreds of steps. Bear Creek is in a quiet, green valley and offers great camping on both sides of the creek.

10. *Laurel Valley access to top of Jocassee/Toxaway*
    13 miles each day. Extremely strenuous; recommended for only the strongest backpackers. Cross through Laurel Valley and up and over "Heartbreak Ridge," widely considered to be the most difficult section of the Foothills Trail. Your reward is excellent campsites with picnic tables, and gorgeous views of Lake Jocassee and the Toxaway River.

Top 10 Day Hikes

Easy

1. *Nicholson Ford Road Access to Pigpen Falls Area*
   About 3 miles round trip, depending on how much explora-
   tion you choose to do. Great for families with children, or
   if you're short on time. In warmer months, enjoy refreshing
   dips in the waterfall pools. Follow signs for Licklog Falls to
   add an extra waterfall on this hike.

Moderate

2. *Nicholson Ford Road Access to Chattooga River Valley*
   6 to 8 miles round trip, depending on where you turn
   around as you walk along the Chattooga River. Highlights
   are waterfalls and the river itself.

3. *Nicholson Ford Road Access to Burrell's Ford Access*
   8.9 miles round trip. Can be hiked in either direction;
   requires either a shuttle driver or one vehicle at the start and
   a second at the other end. Features the entire section of the
   Foothills Trail that follows the Chattooga River.

4. *Laurel Valley Access to Virginia Hawkins Falls*
   9 miles round trip. Not only do you get to see multi-segment-
   ed Virginia Hawkins Falls, you'll also see some of the best of
   the Laurel Valley, a temperate rainforest.

Virginia Hawkins Falls is just off the trail.

HIKING SOUTH CAROLINA'S FOOTHILLS TRAIL

5. *Laurel Valley Access to Sassafras Mountain*
   9.4 miles round trip. It's either all uphill or all downhill on this ascent to and descent from the highest point (3,553 feet) in South Carolina.

Strenuous

6. *Bad Creek to Upper Whitewater Falls*
   4.6 miles round trip. A tough climb to the best view of a dramatic falls plunging over 400 feet. Many rocks and steps on this hike. From Bad Creek Access at the Foothills Trail, follow the signs to Whitewater Falls.

7. *Bad Creek to Thompson River*
   6.8 miles round trip, with perhaps the toughest 5 miles of climbing on the Foothills Trail. You'll cross over two steep mountains to reach beautiful Thompson River.

8. *Bad Creek to Hilliard Falls*
   11.4 miles round trip; even more of the toughest climbing of the Foothills Trail. This hike features big ascents, the roaring Thompson River, Bearcamp Creek, and the finale: 50-foot Hilliard Falls.

9. *Table Rock to Sassafras Mountain*
   9.8 miles. Can be hiked in either direction; requires a shuttle driver or one vehicle at the start and a second at the other end. Hike up through Table Rock State Park's Pinnacle Mountain, past Drawbar Cliffs, and all the way to the highest point in South Carolina at 3,553 feet.
   Note: Table Rock State Park is a fee area.

10. *Table Rock to Pinnacle Mountain (false) Summit*
    7.4 miles round trip. Hike up through Table Rock State Park to one of the best south-facing views in the entire South Carolina Upstate. Optional: continue your hike another 0.8 mile (for a total round trip of 9 miles) to Drawbar Cliffs, with views all the way to Lake Keowee and the Blue Ridge Escarpment. Note: Table Rock State Park is a fee area.

Acknowledgments

This book was literally years in the making, with countless backpacking trips, day hikes, five thru-hikes, and many late nights spent in research and fine-tuning. Without the help and vision of a few key individuals, it would likely still be a campfire discussion topic and a lonely, unfinished manuscript on my computer.

Billy "Monty" Montgomery and I have logged more than three dozen trips on the Foothills Trail and completed a thru-hike together, and for years he persisted in asking me to write this book. Monty, thank you for all your support and encouragement. I'll see you on the trail!

I am indebted to the entire staff at Appalachian Outfitters in Greenville, SC, where I worked for nearly four years. They are truly professional outfitters. More times than I can count, co-owner Jonathan Welsh encouraged me to hit the Foothills Trail on my days off and to "write a better guide." Special thanks also go to Diana Ward and Thea Bader for their encouragement.

Finally, this guidebook would not be in your hands were it not for the vision, direction, and publishing talent of Mary Ellen Hammond and Jim Parham of Milestone Press. They are truly a pleasure to work with and share a love of the outdoors and good trail information.

About the Author

Scott Lynch has been hiking, backpacking, and camping along the trails of the Carolinas since 1989. A business and technical writer who is also the author of *Family Hikes in Upstate South Carolina*, he lives in the South Carolina Upstate.

Milestone Press

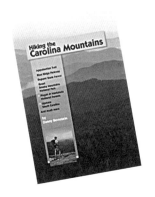
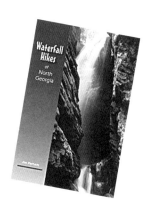

Hiking

- *Backpacking Overnights: NC Mountains, SC Upstate* by Jim Parham

- *Day Hiking the North Georgia Mountains* by Jim Parham

- *Hiking Atlanta's Hidden Forests* by Jonah McDonald

- *Hiking North Carolina's Blue Ridge Mountains* by Danny Bernstein

- *Hiking the Carolina Mountains* by Danny Bernstein

- *Family Hikes in Upstate South Carolina* by Scott Lynch

- *Waterfalls Hikes of North Georgia* by Jim Parham

- *Waterfalls Hikes of Upstate South Carolina* by Thomas E. King

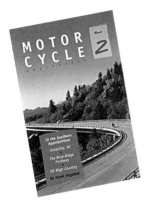

Motorcycle Adventure Series
by Hawk Hagebak

- *1–Southern Appalachians: North GA, East TN, Western NC*

- *2–Southern Appalachians: Asheville NC, Blue Ridge Parkway, NC High Country*

- *3–Central Appalachians: Virginia's Blue Ridge, Shenandoah Valley, West Virginia Highlands*

Mountain Bike Guides
by Jim Parham

- *Mountain Bike Trails— NC Mountains & SC Upstate*

- *Mountain Bike Trails— North GA & Southeast TN*

Milestone Press

Road Bike Guide Series

- *Road Bike Asheville, NC*
  by the Blue Ridge Bicycle
  Club

- *Road Bike North Georgia*
  by Jim Parham

- *Road Bike the Smokies*
  by Jim Parham

Family Adventure

- *Natural Adventures in
  the Mountains of
  North Georgia*
  by Jim Parham &
  Mary Ellen Hammond

Pocket Guides

- *Hiking South Carolina's Foothills Trail* by Scott Lynch

- *Hiking & Mountain Biking DuPont State Forest* by Scott Lynch

- *Hiking & Mountain Biking Pisgah Forest* by Jim Parham

Wildflower Guides

- *Wildflower Walks & Hikes— NC Mountains* by Jim Parham

Can't find the Milestone Press guidebook you want at a bookseller near you? Call us at 828-488-6601 or visit www.milestonepress.com for purchase information.